His Beauty for My Ashes
A Glance Into a Life Christ Saved

Coming Soon from True Vine Publishing

I Hear God In My Head
V.R. Griffin

His Beauty for My Ashes

A Glance Into a Life Christ Saved

S. C. Jamison

True Vine Publishing Company

John 15:5

His Beauty for My Ashes
Published by True Vine Publishing Company
P.O. Box 22448
Nashville, Tennessee 37202

Characters and events mentioned in any short stories within this book are fictional, and any resemblance to actual persons or events is coincidental.

ISBN: 1-932203-79-6

Printed in the United States of America
2004—First printing

To place orders for this book or for more information
On the author or publisher go to **www.TrueVinePublishing.com**

Book layout: Timothy O. Bond

Cover Design: Jimmy Jamison, Jr.., MCP:
Jamison Development Solutions (www.JamisonDevelopment.com)

Cover photo courtesy: Philip Greenspun   (http://philip.greenspun.com)

Back Cover Photo: Emanuel Roland:
Roland's Photography   (www.RolandsPhotographs.net)

Acknowledgements

The manifestation of this book is the direct result of love and support of many people. I acknowledge your faith and encouragement as the very pillars of this book's foundation. I love you and thank you.

To husbands named Jimmy
Whose love captured me at age fifteen
You are my traveling partner
For this road called Life
For better and for worse
I love you
Your dedication to excellence
Your support for this inner desire
To write words that tell stories
Has touched me infinitely

To children named
Trystan, Taylor and Justus
Stepchildren Devon and Jaden
Living life with you
And the knowledge of you
Has caused me to be a new person
With more love than I knew I had

To Moms and Dads named
Gina and Michael
You have been the very best parents
You could be
Or knew to be
I love and thank you for being honest
In everything

To sisters and brothers named Ebony and Michael
If you can take my life
And those of others you have seen
Use the mistakes as lessons
And the good times for laughter
You can live with liberty

To friends named
Ashley, Cheryl, Kendra, Lakeesha,
Robyn, Tera, and Tim
Who brainstorm with me on pen names
Send me books of poets who have stepped out
On this book thing
Who drop off kids at our house and bring inspiration
With them
Who say, "Girl, you know all you wanna do is write."
Tell me I am a "trail blazer" or "you are really going to do great things"
Your words and actions
Have not been lost
But tucked within the inner garment of my inspiration

For churches like
Word of Faith Christian Center-Nashville
And Pastors named
Pastor and Mrs. Henry Coles, Jr. with
Home meetings, prayer groups, and awesome church families
Your support is unspeakably warming
Your love infinitely echoing
Your teaching on how to live life
In His fullest abundance
Has allowed me to pray and love and live
Without constraint

For universities like
Fisk University
With professors named Dr. Moran, Dr. Popkin and Dr. Meyer
Your encouragement
Despite my two pregnancies and marriage
Allowed me to dream
Literary dreams without the stench
Of a dream deferred

Table of Contents

For those who have found themselves in the pit of despair or the wilderness of pain and suffer from the overwhelming loneliness of it all. He is Great and He is Mighty. His Grace waits for you, extending its hand, allowing room for you within its arms.

Walk with me. Walk with me as I tell you my story. As we walk, let my words touch you and their meaning cause you to praise. Praise the Lord and give Him glory. For I present to you, through this collection of poetry, a brief synopsis of my praise report. The ugly is presented only to help you appreciate the beauty. The ugly is always there and we fuss, cuss and complain. But if we can take the time out to say, Glory to God and Amen, well, we have embarked upon a journey to His peace. It has taken me a long time to resign myself and say, Glory to God and Amen, but because of His infinite Mercy and Grace, I am able to say this and believe it. I am handing you a piece of my life's pie, to taste and chew for a minute and it is your decision to swallow or spit it out. It is my prayer, that as you walk with me, through my journey, you will pick up a few pieces of wisdom and serenity on the way. We fuss. We cuss. We complain. We even have messed up peace on the inside but if you look, He is waiting to trade His beauty for your ashes.

Childhood

1

Serenity of wintertime
Falls from gray skies
And lands as feathers
Upon once green grass
The serenity is in its quiet descent
Non-intrusive or demonstrative as sky tears
Or blue exclamation points from the clouds
But peaceful quiet
subtly beautiful
awakening the senses with an occasional brisk wind
the serenity of white feathers
upon once green grass
brings remembrances of sock gloves
two pairs of pants
three sweaters
and laughter
remembrances of living room campouts
with momma and daddy
brother and sister
resting wonderfully
lovingly in quiet warmth
without distractions of anger
or accusation
serenity of wintertime
falls from gray skies
and lands as feathers
upon once green grass
awakening me to child laughter
to present day children who jump up and down
with the excitement of snow time bliss
their mittens and snow hats glistening with
white feathers
bringing smiles of love and peace
and remembrances of winters past

Four-Year-Old Eyes

I saw you with four year old eyes
I sat at your feet and watched you play your keyboard
with headphones and tears streaming
I saw you with four year old eyes
crying silently to a melody
I didn't know
with four year old eyes
you see daddies that are strong
that hold the world up for you to live in
and I saw you crying
you didn't answer when I called to you
when I asked you what was wrong
but you cried silently to the melody of a tune
I didn't know
when I got older and I saw you become a demon
before my very eyes
when you let that evil ugly person come out of you
that made you say mean things and
made you do awful things
I saw you with four year old eyes
but I never asked you what was wrong
because I knew there was no answer
because there was fear in me
and fear in you
now that I am older, grown, with babies of my own,
I see you with four year old eyes still
I question, within the curiosity of my being, why don't you move,
move to the rhythm of normalcy
corporate America
8 to 5
why do you stay imprisoned to the confinements
of your mind
but with four year old eyes I see you still and
with a four year old heart I love you and

I wait and pray for your deliverance
your liberty
the parole of your heart
mind
spirit
I love you more and more
every day

The Fine China of Life - Sestina

Footprints of the heart's beach
Steadfast in the black death of each night
Petrifying, solidifying with dusty pebbles of pain
Shattering innocence, the fine china of life
Rebirths of the long lost
Handprints, that wash away in the orange birth of day.

While mommies with rainbow faces appear in the day
More footprints are scattered across the beach
Mind tells brain the footprints are surely lost
As daddies with long tails and red horns howl to the night
Whispers, sanity, the fine china of life
Broken, shattered with dusty pebbles of pain.

The turning of clock faces, dull stabs of pain
Times tables, verbs, p.e. distract the hours of day
3:30 changes spelling tests to survival tests of life
footprints begin to walk slowly along heart's beach
laughter, jokes, playtime of school day suddenly lost
to screams of mommies and howls of daddies, in the black night.

Sleep comes to the dying of night
After stumbling over tears and dusty pebbles of pain
Footprints of night only subconsciously lost
Amid the I'm sorrys and I love yous of day
Handprints are made upon the heart's beach
As hugs, kisses and making babies, again become, the fine china of
life.

Kisses, whispers, laughter, the fine china of life
Protect, comfort through the death of each night
Handprints replace footprints along the heart's beach
And dusty pebbles of pain
Hide from the orange births of day

With the footprints, that are only subconsciously lost.

The turning of clock faces proves nothing is ever lost,
Only hidden. Hiding, the finest china of life
Tucked under covers of laughter and sheets of day
Sometimes uncovered by the howls of night
Sometimes bruised by dusty pebbles of pain
Always solidifying in the sands of the heart's beach.

Footprints of the heart's beach are never lost to distractions of day
Or the turning clocks of life. They are hidden beneath piles of
Dusty pebbles of pain, in the black death of each night.

Gemma Williams

i don't know where you are
or where your hiding place
is in the world
gemma williams.
but i wonder
where you have found
your self.
are you the little girl
with string yellow hair
and the faded jeans with the hole
that you wore on mondays
tuesdays thursdays fridays
and who said
my daddy screws horses?
where are you gemma
or where have you found
your self?
did you miss the prom
or were you queen?
do you have babies
or degrees?
are you still a genius
pretending to be dumb and slow?
i just wonder gemma
because i have found
me and life and love.
our stimulating talks
of beaten mothers
and crazy fathers
in fifth grade lunch lines
with the long orange lunch tickets
and pockets with only lint
for rice krispy treats and ice cream
have danced with me in dreams

and sometimes
i just think about you
and wonder
where you have found your self
gemma williams.

Peace Be Still
(After an Attack of Remembering and Reliving)

Oh God oh God
Give me peace
Give me quiet
Give me whispers
Oh God

Eyes jump open
At the shattering of glass
And *oh God, please don't*
Feet and legs kick
Off bedspread and sheet
And scamper to the living room
As heart races
Thumpety thump
Thumpety thump
And mind says
Please don't let her die tonight
As I stand
In front of the picture
That will haunt my mind
In the death of each night
That picture worth more
Than her echoing screams
Daddy strangling
Hitting
Cocking his rifle
Call the police!
Don't call the police or I really will
Kill her!
Daddy stop!
Please stop!
Feet scamper to the bedroom
To hush crying babies
To pray

Our Father, which art in heaven
Don't let our daddy kill our mommy
Please God…please God…please…
Wake up wake up wake up
Its ok its ok its ok
I'm not him
Focus on me I'm not him
You are at home
I'm not him
Oh God oh God
Give me peace
Give me quiet
Give me whispers

Give me peace
Give me quiet
Give me whispers
Oh God

Him
is rehabilitated
and cannot remember
hell on earth
her is in denial
and will not remember
hell on earth

I am facing
The demons of remembrance
On my own
Oh God oh God
Give me peace
Give me quiet
Give me whispers

Family

2

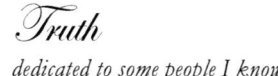

Truth

dedicated to some people I know

The very essence of purity that maintains our completeness
our being whole
our life's strength
truth
we run from his eyes
try to hide behind
denial's smoke screens
but truth
never leaves never runs away
just stands there until
we are ready to take him
embrace him
wear him as a part of our life

Truth is
loving you
loving you enough to tell you
I don't like when you hit me or
call me four letter words
that are too dirty to utter
because it hurts
it hurts on the outside and
it hurts down on the inside
way down there
where I hold my love for me

Truth is
loving you
loving you enough to tell you that
I don't like when you look out the windows and
talk to people I don't know and
you don't know or
when you see people
I can't see and you laugh with them

hold private conversations with them
then look at me
as though I am a stranger and
I am your daughter or your niece

Truth is
loving you
loving you enough to tell you
I have learned words are eternal pieces of life and death
you can't curse me from my eyelashes
to my toenails in one breath and
in the other say I Love You or Praise the Lord, Hallelujah and
expect me to feel warm tingly love feelings for you

Truth is
loving you
loving you enough to tell you
I have learned life is not about
the boys on the street,
the laced sticks of instant-high you smoke,
the cognac you drink,
the sport of running from the police or
being a thug or
loving a thug

Truth is
loving you
loving you enough to tell you that
I am not impressed with
who you know or who you are,
how much money they have or is supposed to give you,
where you go to eat or who you meet,
how big your ring is or where you live,
how much authority you exert or control you keep

Truth is
loving you
loving you enough to tell you that
I am going to be me
from now until eternity and
that is no freak accident or flaw in design
but I am whole and like being me and
everything He has created in me and

Truth is
loving you
loving you enough to tell you
while the world keeps moving
telling you while we stand
in the present time,
the present day
so that you will hear and take the present day
and do something different.

Truth is breaking the cycle of erroneous repetition.
Consider yourself told.
Consider yourself loved.

Monday Mornings, Friday Nights

My eyes model
brown stockings
in white pumps
when the sun smiles
and daddy laughs
at the editorials.

My eyes don
red scarves
and clear jellies
when the sun hides
and daddy curses
the funny papers

My brother told me
I love you
Today
Without any announcement
Or forewarning
He told me
He loved me as he secretly
Left five dollars
In my car ashtray
He told me
He loved me
Young boy of seventeen
Who has not seen
The great beauties
Nor the great evils
Of this place: Life.
But has only tasted
The fruits of both
Oh beautiful heart
Innocent one
Don't be lost to the temptations
Of darkness
Continue to let your beauty
Blossom to greatness
You have warmed my soul
And lifted my heart
Thank you for
"worryin about me sometime"
and making me smile
speechless tears
to the tune of your
I love yous

Mom, I Love You

Do you love me?
Yes, I love you.
Do you love me?
Yes, I love you.

I love you more
Than new bikes on Christmas
Dollar bills for lost teeth
Snuck under my pillow
In the quiet of night
I love you more
Than chocolate cake and ice cream
At the genesis of the month
I love you more and more and more
With each day of fresh mercy
Because now
I am a Mommy and share
This Mother title with you
And I understand
How big how wide how deep
Your shoes are
And with all of me my effort my time
And my talents
I can not fill your shoes
Or cause them to overflow
Because I have not attempted
Superwoman feats
Nor challenged evil in it's face
Nor sat at the feet of endurance
Or longsuffering
I have not stood in the middle of chaos
And declared with the persistence
Of waking up every morning
That indeed there will be peace

Do you love me?
Yes, I love you.
Do you love me?
Yes, I love you.

I love you so much
That I pray for your laughter
That it would reach your eyes
And comfort your soul
Laughter, real laughter
The kind that makes your smile hurt
I love you so much
That I pray for clock faces to turn
And turn and turn for eternity in your favor
That your clock won't stop until the sky splits
Or you are ready to go home
I love you so much
i pray that you enjoy life's chocolate
That you take the time to smell it's sweet temptation
Taste the savor of exhilaration, the joy of life's chocolate

Do you love me?
Yes, I love you.
Do you love me?
Yes, I love you.

More than words could ever write.

Dare You
To Daddy

"Dare you to lift yourself up off the floor. Dare you to move."
                              -Dare you to Move, Switchfoot

I dare you to take a chance on Life
Explore its contents without fear
Or panic attacks or demons
That entertain the thoughts that communicate
With your mouth…

I dare you to move, to trust
Someone to help you from the paralysis
Time has imprisoned you in…

I dare you to love, love the people around you
To talk to them of past wrongs and hurts
The very inexplicable…

I dare you to move, move
MOVE
Please move, step away from that door
Entering into eternal torment…

I dare you…
I dare you to move

Girl
You are so fly
You possess your own style
Your own flava
Delighting in the practical areas of life
Saving money
Paying bills on time
Being honest in everything
And yet
You play in the red zones
Associating with drama and
Situations filled with the dramatic
Conforming to no one's ideals
But your own
Your love emerges in tight hugs
And fights for what it knows
Late night talks with you
And a cup of tears
Or daytime chats
on borrowed employer's time
bind my heart to yours
you are my inspiration
to be a good big sister
to tell you of all the crooks
and nannies of this road Life
so you don't make the mistakes
that have haunted me or caused me despair
You are a breath of hip hop
With the sensitivity of classical
And the warmth of jazz
Looking for your place
In the middle of everyone else's
perspective

To Mike

Thank you for coming out to see me
On those days I get to feeling
Lonely on the inside
Thank you for feeling me
Thinking of me
To just drop by
You are priceless
A pearl even
Because you are still
afraid of the dark
And you cry
When the pain is too much
And because you haven't learned
How to hide behind the harshness
Of being a man
I love you endlessly
Thank you.

I drove to the house boosting up my inner strength by affirming the good things about her. Remembering warm caramel colored coffee that she allowed me to sip on Saturday mornings, quickened the admiration I held for her. On weekend sleepovers, I used to think she stayed up all night because she was always awake on my way to slumber's hideout. She was also awake when I found morning's sun as a companion. She was strength. As I sat in front of the white house with the porch meant for rocking chairs, I willed myself to enjoy my visit with her. I willed myself to look past the cancer-ridden body and see the woman who sipped warm caramel colored coffee at the kitchen table. I willed myself to see strength.

Everyone who was normally at the house taking care of Grandmomma was out today running errands. I guess they decided to take advantage of my visit and to experience life outside of 1114 Granada Avenue. I sat in the quiet house for awhile and listened to the low hum of the a.m. gospel radio station.

"Shamica?"
"Yes, ma'am?"
"It's time to go. I got to go. They waitin' on me."
"Huh, Grandmomma?"
"I've got to go. It's time to go"

I looked at the sight in front of me in awe. My grandmother, reduced to the puny size of 6 from a womanly size of 18, lay there paralyzed. From her left shoulder to her left toe, she couldn't move and yet…she said she had to go.

"Grandmomma, Momma didn't tell me that you had somewhere to go. Do you need or want me to do something for you?"

"Baby," she says this real patient-like, "get my white dress hangin' on the door, my knee-high socks and my white shoes. I'm gone need someone to comb my hair but I got to go. They waitin' on me".

I looked on the door of her room and sure enough, there lay the white dress. It was pressed neatly among the other dresses hanging there.

"My knees hi's are over here in this drawer next to the bed".

"Huh?" I didn't say this because I didn't hear her. I said it as if to say, *Woman what you talkin' bout? You haven't gone anywhere in months, where do you have to go? Why didn't Momma tell me she had a doctor's appointment today? I can't lift her out of the bed and into regular clothes! Maybe if I just sit here and be real quiet, maybe she won't say anything else.*

"Shamica?" No response.
"Shamica??" No response.
"SHAMICA????"
"HUH?"
"You gettin' my stuff together? They waitin' on me. I got to go."
"Grandmomma, who's waitin?"
"*They* waitin?!"
Oooh weee. She is upset now! I can't let Momma come back and Grandmomma has worked herself into a fit. Momma will have my head! Where is everybody? Didn't nobody tell me she had an appointment. Where does she have to go anyway? Wait a minute…she dosen't have to go anywhere…this visit is not working the way I planned it to.

"GinaSharonJoniEbony…Shamica! Get the dress off the door and get my shoes!"
She is as hot as fiery crystals! I have got to do something. Ok, if I put on

her knee hi's, maybe she will calm down...

"Ok, Grandmomma, I'ma get your shoes and your knee hi's!"

We went back and forth with this ping pong game of wills for about fifteen minutes and then there was silence. Grandmomma had stopped talking to me by the time Momma got there.

"How was your visit," Momma asked.

"It was good," I replied as I started to pack up my book bag. Momma and I chatted for a few minutes, never delving into the actual conversation Grandmomma and I had experienced. I left for the dorm, turning over in my head what the right thing was to do for the situation that just transpired.

Two days later, grandmother departed this life and began her journey on the eternal one. It seems as though she really had somewhere to go, after all. As I cried with the thought of her absence, I prayed she would forgive my disobedience to her requests; the seeming disregard for her urgency.

I think of Grandmomma on Saturday mornings, as my house and its inhabitants sleep. I think of her during weekday bustles as I drink sweet warm coffee and savor its aroma. I think of her and know that she smiles at me from her heavenly kitchen table. I imagine her sitting there serenely, tipping her cup to me.

To My Girls, With Love

To my girls
my feel-like flesh and blood sisters
my snotty shouldered tissue bearers
my comedy club
my heart and soul with pride
hollerin, "That's MY GIRL!"
I love ya'll and
Ya'll love me

I love you so much that
when you cry that gut wrenchin' cry
my insides go twisty turvy
when you walk across that stage
with all those honors and accolades
my heart swells up
with that momma kinda pride
because I know what it took
to make that walk

when you get those promotions
and phat raises
my ears ring with hallelujahs
like the angels were singing
right above my head
because I know too
the hardships of a tight week

when you buy that new car
get the new crib
find Mr. Right for real
I feel like running with joy
because you deserve all the blessings
He has to give

Ladies
because I love you
with the ugly tears
I wanted you to know
it doesn't matter how many
trails you blaze
or life events you initiate
if you don't have love
or the salvation of His blood
it is all
null and void

To my girls
my feel-like flesh and blood sisters
my snotty shouldered tissue bearers
my comedy club
my heart and soul with pride
hollerin, "That's MY GIRL!"
I love ya'll and
I know
Ya'll love me

Marriage

3

yeah
well you know
his union
this togetherness
this for better or for worse till death do you part i'm gone eat with you
sleep with you wake up in the morning and look at you for the rest of my
life thing
is like riding
one of those outside elevators
that go up real high
and real fast
and you get a rush just by looking at the city
right beside you
but you also get real scared
cause you don't know
when or where or how its gonna stop
yeah
this is what that eternal contract
signed by us
witnessed by the state
and bonded by God
feels like
yeah
but you know
its cool
i can dig it
because
the times that he feels
like eddie murphy
are the times that i look like
a potbellied don king
and we laugh
and feel that rush of going higher
and higher

or the times
when we sit together
on the green porch
in the green lawn chairs
and watch the clouds
flirt with the moon
as the wind sings their favorite song
and we get that feeling
you know
of quiet and whispers
and of slowly going higher but its okay because we have each other to
hold on to forever and ever
and we just talk
yeah
and you know
this for better or for worse till death do you part i'm gone eat with you
sleep with you wake up in the morning and look at you for the rest of
my life thing
gets pretty scary
a lot of the times
because
the elevator ride isn't always smooth
and sometimes
it doesn't always soar to the top
but kinda drops a few floors
and makes your heart skip like a c.d.
and your knees get a tingly fluttery sensation
yeah
and you know there are times
when we only have the smell
of gas in the gas tank
and a $1.50 between us
until payday
which is six days away

and we get to thinking about
our 1.5 kids and how and why did we do this and our age combined does
not even equal up to 45 and the cable'll be cut off tomorrow if we don't
come up with this month's last month's and next month's bill
and then
i cry
i cry because
my tummy is stretching into a big brown basketball, i am beginning to
waddle like a big brown duck, my name isn't tyra banks, and i wasn't
chosen to be one of victoria's secrets supermodel angels
and then
he cries
he cries because
he wasn't born with bill gates or michael jordan
printed on his birth certificate
and you know
its okay
because we cry
together
and this for better or for worse till death do you part i'm gone eat with
you sleep with you wake up in the morning and look at you for the rest of
my life thing
becomes
so real
and then you wonder
you know
when and if and how
the elevator will stop
and then you get kinda scared
but then
that rush floods through your body
all the way
from your toenails
to your eyelashes

yeah
and then
he points out
that i have on
three shades of green
black socks and white shoes
and i point out
that he has
a friend in his nose
and then
you know
we laugh
and take all 6 quarters
along with the 75 pennies
that we borrowed from the baby's bank
and proudly hand them
to the cashier at speedway
(you know the one with the cheap gas)
and we laugh some more.
yeah.
this for better or for worse till death do you part i'm gone eat with you
sleep with you wake up in the morning and look at you for the rest of
my life thing
is cool
and you know
i can dig it
yeah.

I came home and you told me
You **told** me
Straight from your three-year-old soul
You are daddy's life
You marry him and kiss him and
You are daddy's **life**
Of course this was news
That hope, that inspiration, that
I hope she can be right in her three-year-old wisdom
But upon closer inspection of three-year-old grammar
With two tears from my right eye
And three from the left
Along with a little swelling of anticipation
Sprinkled in a little
Adult comprehension
I realized that you
You were just repeating
A fact
And not a wonder
Because what you were
Really trying to tell me was
You are daddy's **wife**
However
Little one with so much knowledge
And eyes of wisdom
It pains me to tell you
I have been neither
For a really long time.

Confrontation

After weeks or was it months of stillness silence
Avoidance of each other's presence
After living in the same space and sleeping in the same bed but
never connecting
Never loving never hearing or conversing
but yelling and avoiding
your words reverberated against the walls with
I have something to tell you
And I knew it was coming just as you can anticipate a slap in the
face but never knowing how long the sting will echo upon your face
that is how I sat awaiting what I believed would be the end
It was a day in May
the first week of May, matter of fact and you told me of the baby
that was on its way
The father you had become in evening absences from our home
when you were supposed to be at a friend's or playing ball
You told me that you hadn't been the husband you should have
But instead had been following another life walking in another per-
son's shoes and as I sat there holding my breath waiting for the
words "I don't love you anymore"
I sat there very still so that when the words came I could breathe my
despair into one great breath but
They never came
And I told you about the affection the attention the time I had
given to another, the affair that I participated in, the wife I had not
been
Instead you said you needed some time, we needed some time apart
and
I believed we had hope because you never said the words, you never
said you didn't want me or the babies anymore and I had hope and
thought this could be worked out; what I believed could be fixed in
two weeks ended up being nine months

I sat on the couch
I ate corn from the can
I watched Nick at Nite

As I became a robot of habit
Forfeiting warm meals from the oven
For the solace of crisp sweet corn
Straight from the can
Asserting my independence
By boycotting warm meals from the stove
I sat on the couch and watched the Jeffersons
move on up and Archie Bunker scream into the tube

I reminisced of late night conversations
With you and longed
For you to say
I'm coming home
I ate corn from the can
And watched Nick at Nite
Contemplating what she had
That was better
Than what I offered
Turned over in my head
How I could be prettier
Little more sassy
Little more confident
A little more like her

I sat on the couch
I ate corn from the can
I watched Nick at Nite
And I missed you
My best friend
The vessel for all of my secrets

My very life line
To all that was good
Happy
Worthy of laughter
I sat on the couch
I ate corn from the can
I watched Nick at Nite
I got angry
Mesmerizing angry
At your audacity
To father children
Without me
But most of all
Betraying all that I had given you
Mesmerizing angry
Because I gave you all
The love I had to give

I sat on the couch
I ate corn from the can
I watched Nick at Nite
Wondering how you lived life
As a bachelor
When I had babies
That still cried in the night

I sat on the couch
I ate corn from the can
I watched Nick at Nite
And slept with the incandescence
Of lamp light
Replacing your body warmth
With the security of light
Crying at the thought

That your scent will never
Touch my pillow as a companion again

I sat on the couch
I ate corn from the can
I watched Nick at Nite
After I went to that lawyers office
Collected legal long papers
Confused at the legal complexities
Of the English language
Feeling as though
I took your place
In the betrayal game

I sat on the couch
I ate corn from the can
I watched Nick at Nite
While you were gone

Forgiveness

4

Forgiveness comes with
Still morning-time suns after
Rain shower sunsets

I Saw Love

Dedicated to my Husband

My heart plunged then swelled
and I thought whatever I have to do
to keep pain
anguish
disappointment
from your front door
I would fight to make sure
you never smelled the stench of broken dreams
shattered hearts
or loneliness, the pure solitude of loneliness
that quiet insanity of your own thoughts
I would give
everything for you

You wear light-up sneakers
and say
I can do it by myself Mommy
and then spill the gallon of milk
onto the linoleum floor
as you hurry to watch
Saturday morning Loonies
Doras
yellow sponges with pink friends named Patrick
You are marvels
awe inspiring delights
that bring depth to hum drum
carpool routines
non-washable paint stained laundry
ketchup mustard skewered dishes
Ponytailed wonders
you skip to the music
of angels that play nonstop in your spirit
You are faith warriors
who pray non-believing or let's say
Kinda doubting parents into new cars or houses
and out of harms way of bouncing checks
you have sat in hospital rooms with machines
that made Mommy scared
looked them right into their beeping
flashing eyes and said
Holy Spirit is here
Two ponytailed
light up sneaker wearing
cartoon watching girls that whisper
five and seven year old secrets
long past bedtime
You have been sent here
on assignment

from the Most High
and Heavenly place
to teach a Mommy and Daddy
how to say
I love you
no matter what
to be mindful of what
we let our eyes see
and wary of what
our ears hear
to wait, to be still
to be ok with today's grilled cheese
in anticipation of tomorrow's
Filet mignon
Ponytailed wonders
who affirm their independence with
I can do it Mommy,
I sit in my Mommy knowledge
given to me for this journey with you
and think
Yes you can

Oh Love
I hear
Oh Love
I see
Oh Love
I feel you
I am here
I steadied the hand that hit
I guided the bullet that entered
I ordained
That there would be Life
And not death
Oh Love
I answered
Oh Love
I would not
Did not
Leave you alone
I was there
Oh Love
It is not over
Our Father
Sits upon the throne
And is still in control
There are no scars
I can not heal
No memories
I can not erase
No demons
I can not overtake
For you
Love, I am not finished
My work here
Is not done

Not until you see the victory
The battle, the war
Is already won

I put Jesus down
When I heard the preacher
Preach the same sermon
When church became a circus
When I felt more healing
Through Bud Light
Tea from Long Islands
Black and Mild Cigars
With a few packs of Salems
To complete the high
Not to mention
The smooth mind trips
Mary's joints would provide
I put Jesus down
While I laid in unknown beds
In the arms of a strange man
Whose last name I didn't share
I put Jesus down
And with the scarf of pride
That so lovely adorned my neck
I created a noose of burdens
Strongholds
Barriers of pain
I did not want to face
I put Jesus down
Or at least
I thought I had
In the scope of reality's lens
He actually picked me up
He waited for me
On the curb of iniquity
He waited for me
When I cried out
Finally out of my weariness

Out of the exhaustion of being me
He picked me up
He whispered in my ear
The best I love you
I have ever heard
He picked me up
He drove me to the place
Of never turning back
Repentance
And as I stood there
On this road
In this place
Repentance
He held my hands
My hands
Dirty from the soot of rejection
Gritty with debris of heart's pain
He held my hands
Turning them over gently
Into His
He held my hands and slowly
Wiped the pain away
Replacing it with His love
As I looked upon my hands
I saw the supernatural transfer
He traded me
His beauty
For my ashes

Liberty

5

I am so free that I can flow like running water from the faucet and my words that are infused with light and knowledge of past lives and past dreams and past pain it all becomes as distant as the pen from the paper I am so free that I can live I can live with open windows and wear different colored underwear and I can say anything I want because I don't live in the bondage of blanket covered windows and ice skating on my words waiting on the ambush of anger and bitterness to overcome me when the ice breaks I am free and I do what I want and say what I want and I go where I want because I don't worry about my keys being hid or the doors being locked where I can't get out because I am free I am free I am free and I will be free from this day forward because whom the Son sets free is free indeed I am free and my heart does not beat fast in the death of each night in anticipation of floor pacers who speak to voices that I can not hear and I do not live my life in fear because of what I can not see or anticipate

Life Rhythm

Follow the rhythm to the beat of my life
Follow the rhythm to the beat of my life
Follow the rhythm to the beat
Thumpety thump thumpety thump
Heart races to beats of mommies with rainbow faces
And daddies that howl to full moons and dark places
Wondering, praying for Beaver's parents and Gidget's life
And the haha laughter of reality, reality's high life
Thumpety thump thump thumpety thump
Finding sweet love in the caresses of boyfriend angels
Believing this love
This warm tingly I cant wait to see you and your
Believing this was my God and He was my God and
Giving him God priviledges

Thou shalt have no other gods before me

Follow the rhythm to the beat of my life
Follow the rhythm to the beat of my life
Follow the rhythm to the beat
Thumpety thump thumpety thump
Heart racing wondering how the slice of my wrist
Will feel to the waving sensation
Of warm water
After contemplating sleepless nights in a husband's bed
And then choosing to run to foreign arms and unknown beds
Following the rhythm to the beat of my life
Following the rhythm to the beat of my life
Following the rhythm to the beat
Tired so   very   tired of life   and the decisions I have made
Or the answers that were already selected for me
Tired   so very tired
Following the rhythm   until the rhythm stops

I   Love   You
        I have always loved you
I   Love   You
        I have always loved you

Captures my breath
        My attention
My weary loneliness

New beat new rhythm new beat new rhythm new beat new rhythm
new beat new rhythm

I love you
I have been waiting
For you to follow my lead instead of the rhythm of your pain
I AM
That I AM
All knowing
All powerful
All peace
All hearing
Your all

Follow the rhythm of a new beat
My beat My grace My drops of tear blood on wooden crosses for
you
My love for you was My Life
New beat new rhythm new beat new rhythm new beat new rhythm
new beat new rhythm
New love
New rhythm
New peace
New rhythm
New hope

New rhythm
Thumpety thump thump thumpety thump

Now my beat flows to the melody of love uncompromised love un-
censored love strength

Look into my eyes
Into the depths of my soul
And say you don't know me
Allow me to bleed for you
Hang for you
Die for you
And then turn your back
On me
And I will still love you
You saw you heard
You touched
And then you let go
Being alone
I was renewed
And I persevered
And fought for you my love
And even then
I forgave
I looked into the smile of death
And my heart swelled
With the thought
Of you my precious

Worship 1.

You are the very sustenance of my being
You allow my inhaling my exhaling
the very blood flow is maintained
by Your ordination of it all and You call me friend
How awesome You are
so sweet and with a love that makes me
break into a smile as I drive along freeways and think
that You gave me another day
another breath
to exalt Your glory.
who am I, what am I, that You are mindful of me
to make You think of me as You endured a cross?
My love for You grows with deeper revelation
of how small I am and how great You are
I am brought to little words when I think of You and
I love You so big that I can't hold it all
for You are the Christ and I breathe because of Your love and
I exist for Your most divine presence
I am brought to little words to describe You in your finest
speechless almost and You stand near holding out Your hand
to catch me if I should fall
just as I reach out my hand to hold my babies
You extend your eternal intercessions for me
oh how great Thou Art

Laughter sings sweetly
To rose bud awakenings
On dew filled mornings

Heaven's Playroom

Have you danced
With your Lord
Or held
your Master's hand?

In the quiet
Warm recesses
Of Heaven's playroom
the Lamb sits
Who lived
Breathed
As God robed in man

And I have had the most blissful chance
to laugh with Him
wipe His tears
tell Him
I would live
Work as a soldier
In His great army
I am as fallible
as David
As questioning
as Moses
Even doubting
as Thomas
But my heart
My heart has turned
Toward Him
Across my desire
Around my flesh
And straight past my
Intellect
I have seen places

Known things
Sat with Him
As He held
My hand
And talked gently
To me in the quiet recesses
Of Heaven's playroom

Worship 2

For You are great
For You are mighty
For You are great
For You are mighty
For You took the stars
And assigned their seating
Amongst the dark
You placed a fire ball of light
That maintains our warmth
And placed it in the heavenlies
For You intermingled my life
With that of others
So that my obedience
Can yield their deliverance
There are times
When I find myself
Engulfed under the blanket of pressure
Things to do
People to please
That I find You
Understand that You
Are my source
My strength
My very heart beat and breath
You ordained my inhaling and exhaling
And verified it with
"It is good"
You have supernaturally restored
All of my brokenness
Incompleteness
And shown me a love
Infinitely rewarding
You have given me the gifts
Of my children's laughter

My husband's love
With time to enjoy them both
You have shown me
After all the drama has come
And gone
You are still seated
Upon the throne
For You are great
For You are mighty
For You are great
For You are mighty

Prayer of Salvation

Jesus, I need You.
I need You to take me
Shape me
Mold me into
The vessel
You have called me to be.
Come into my heart
And take residence.
Come into my life
And lead the way.
Save me from this life's afflictions
And eternity's torment.
I need You to help my heart to heal
Help my mind renew
Help my flesh
To line up with the Word of God.
I now forgive
The transgressions of others
That I may delight
In the light of Your forgiveness.
Right now
In this moment
I open my heart to You.

To order more Books

Contact
True Vine Publishing Co.
P. O. Box 22448
Nashville, TN. 37202
c/o S. C. Jamison

Please Send _____ # of Books to

Name: _____

Address: _____

_____

_____

Book: $10.00
$2.00 Postage

His Beauty for My Ashes
A Glance Into a Life Christ Saved

S. C. Jamison

True Vine Publishing Co.
P.O. Box 22448
Nashville, TN 37202

Getting "The Word" Out

WWW.TRUEVINEPUBLISHING.COM